THE INCREDIBLY VULGAR AND DEPRAVED COLORING BOOK FOR ADULTS

EAT SHIT,
ASSHOLE

SUCK
MY
TITS

CHOKE ON THIS DICK

BLOWJOB
PRINCESS

SQUIRTER

YES,
DADDY

FILL ME
WITH
CUM

DICK
TASTES
YUMMY

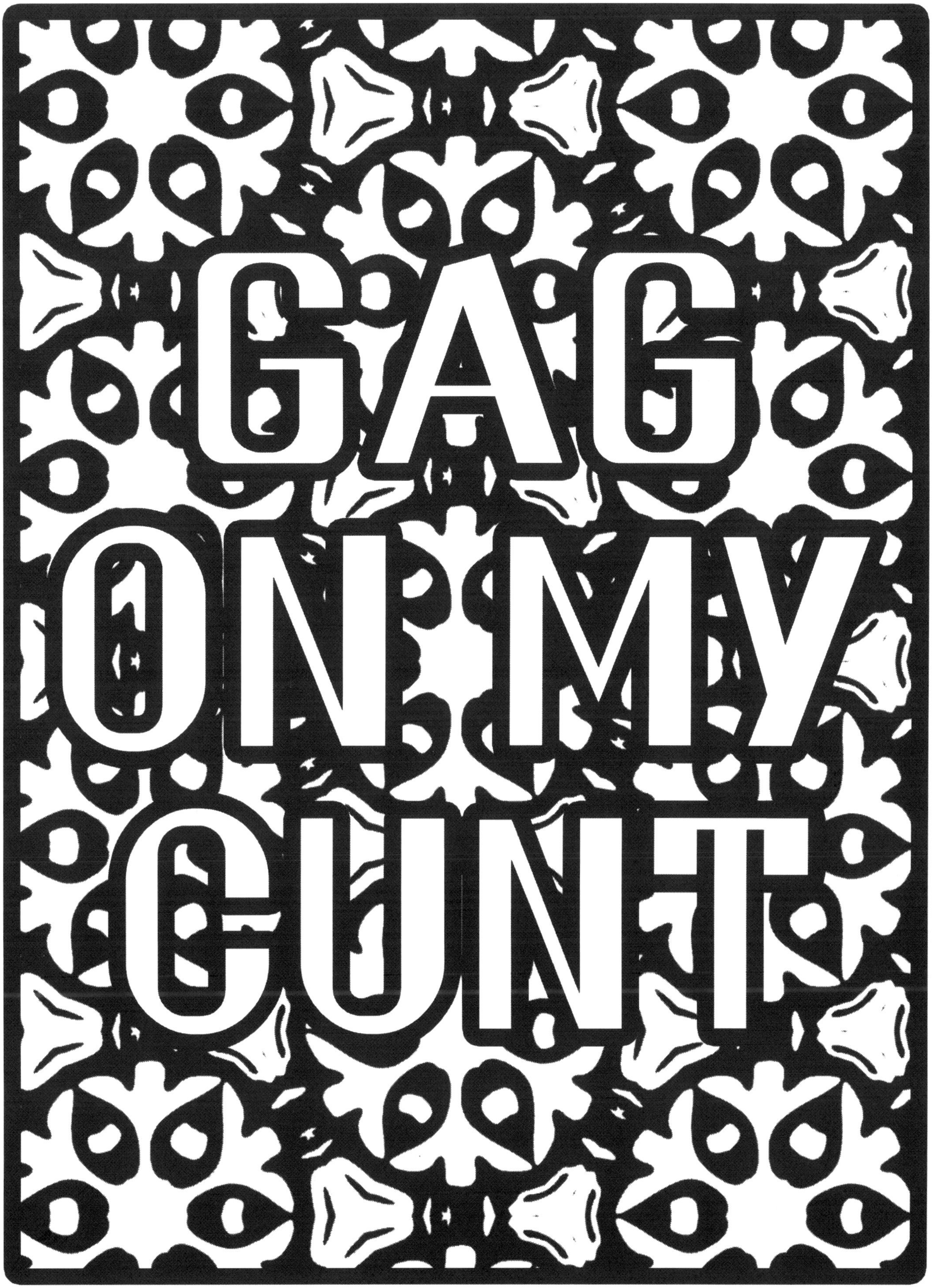
GAG
ON MY
CUNT

DIRTY
FUCKING
SLUT

SUCK
MY
ASS

PEG
ME

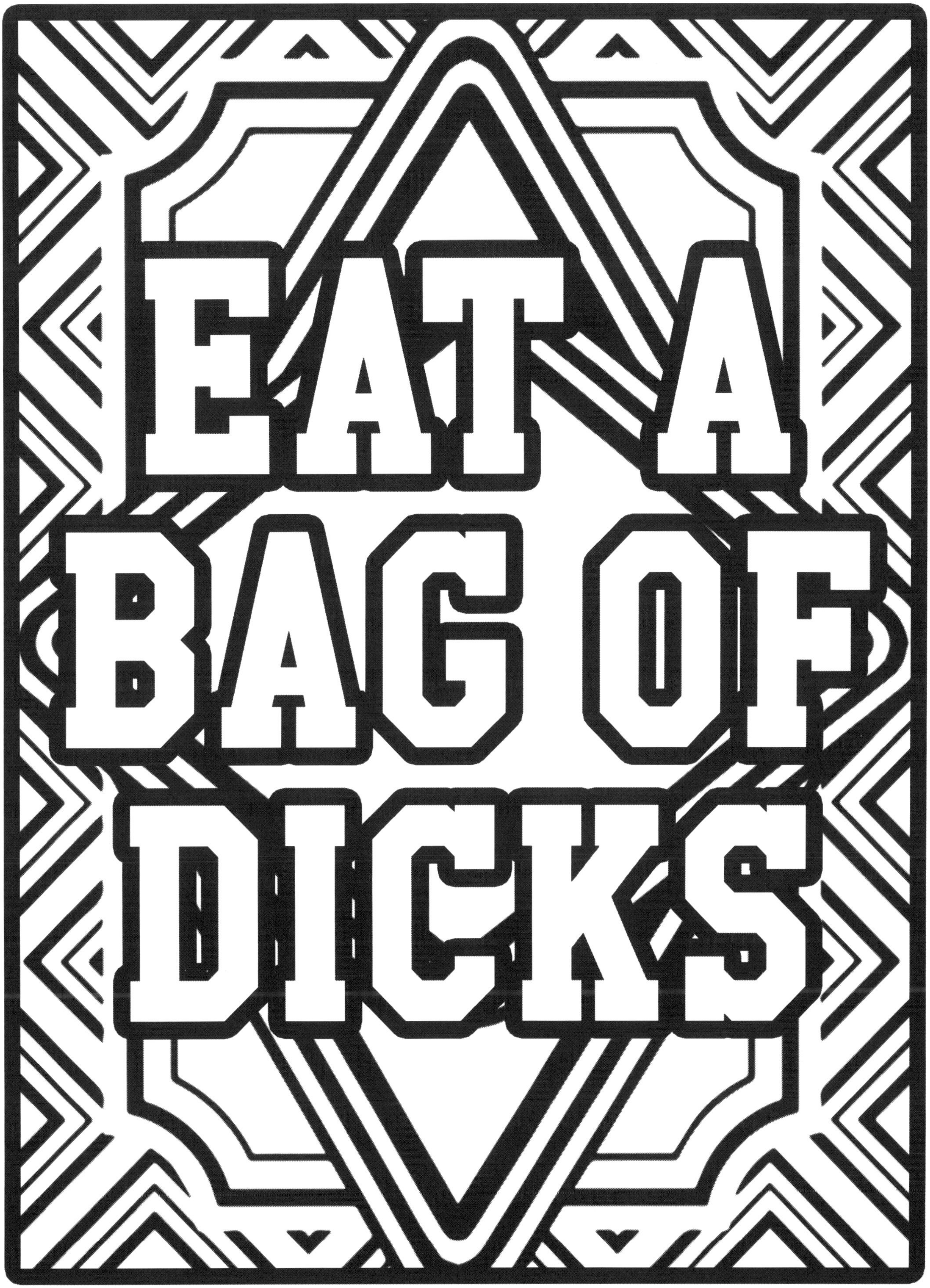
EAT A
BAG OF
DICKS

FUCK
FUCKITY
FUCK
FUCK
FUCK

COCK
SMOKER

SUCK
MY
CUNT

MORE
ANAL
BEADS
PLEASE

LICK ON
SOME
DICK

SWALLOW
MY CUM

ASSHOLE
CLEANER

DADDY'S
PRINCESS

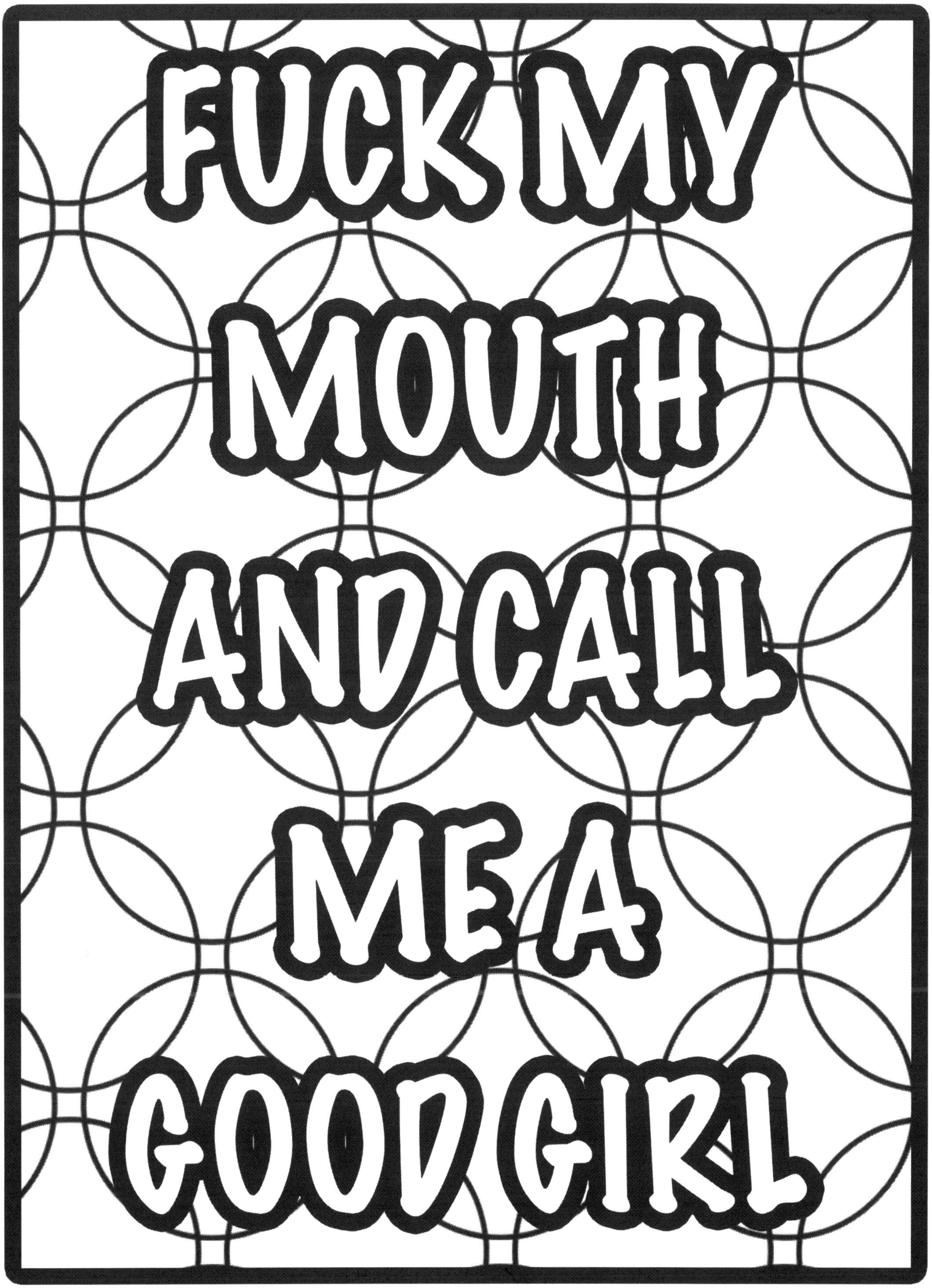
FUCK MY
MOUTH
AND CALL
ME A
GOOD GIRL

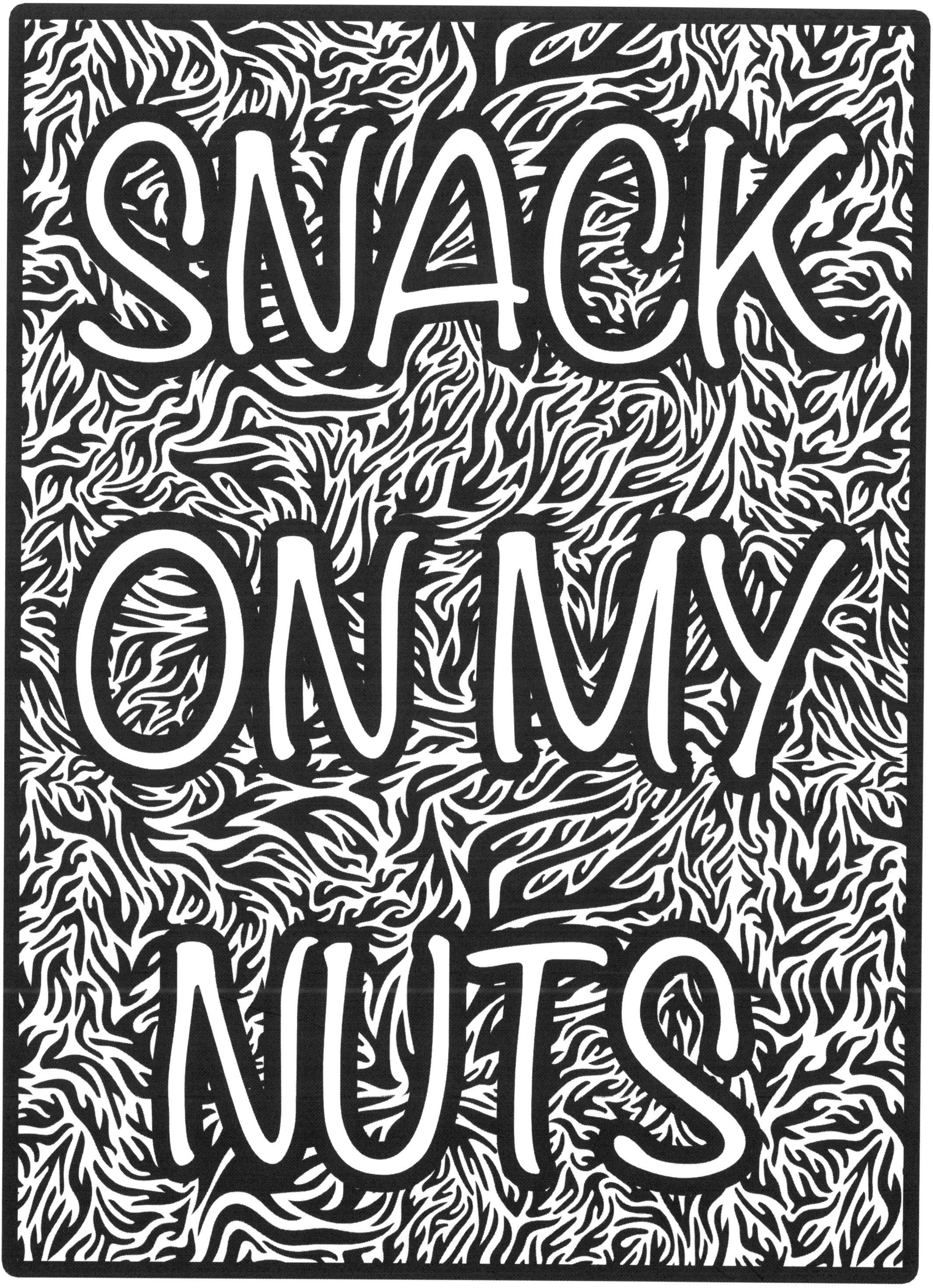
SNACK
ON MY
NUTS

I CUM
FROM
ANAL

ADDICTED
TO THE
PUSSY